MUSCLE TRUCKS

HIGH-PERFORMANCE PICKUPS

Mike Mueller

Iconografix

Iconografix
PO Box 446
Hudson, Wisconsin 54016 USA

Library of Congress Control Number: 2007927570

ISBN-13: 978-1-58388-197-2
ISBN-10: 1-58388-197-2

07 08 09 10 11 12 6 5 4 3 2 1

Printed in China

Cover and book design by Dan Perry

Copyedited by Andy Lindberg

CONTENTS

ACKNOWLEDGMENTS

As usual, I owe many thanks to the many people who made this project possible. I've been writing and photographing automotive history books for nearly 20 years now, and through it all I've had one person I've always known I could count on for a helping hand: my brother, and best friend, Dave Mueller, of Bondville, Illinois. He's been on so many photo shoots with me he now knows my next move before I do. And he's also well versed in what comes last—usually Miller time.

In recent years another brother, Jim Mueller, Jr., of Mahomet, Illinois, has also stepped up to make my job much easier. Jim has set me up with more photo subjects than I can count, and he too knows how to end a work (if photographing cars and trucks can be called that) day in appropriate fashion. Additional help on various shoots came from my sister Kathy's husband, Frank Young (also of Mahomet), who too knows a little about what I do. Or what I don't do—like pick up the check for Monical's pizza. My parents, Jim and Nancy Mueller, of Champaign, Illinois, deserve a kudo or two as well for putting up with me during so many photo junkets to the Midwest. Thanks too, ma, for the mountain of tacos. They're always appreciated.

I also must thank my new family, the McGees, of Kennesaw, Georgia, who recently took me in to raise, keeping me well fed (and well hydrated) during this book's production. Elizabeth McGee and her lesser half Jason have yet to turn me away, or at least they haven't tried hard enough. Daughter Hannah and son Matt-Matt don't seem to mind me around at all, either. Paybacks are on the way, folks.

Additional thanks go to former Ford SVT man John Clor, who for some reason still answers the phone whenever I come begging. The same goes for Chrysler Historical's Brandt Rosenbusch. I've yet to talk to Michael Hood, founder of the Georgia Syclone-Typhoon club. But his timely e-mails helped me meet up with fellow turbo truck enthusiast John Waller, who in turn helped me photograph Lee Dyke's super-cool, super-fast Syclone.

Various other gracious people allowed me to run off with various other photographic subjects from various dealerships in the Midwest. John Thornton, of John Thornton Chevrolet in Lithia Springs, Georgia, actually let me take his own 2006 Chevrolet SSR, a black beauty that I'll always remember touring around in topless. Mike Crews, at Ridings Jeep-Dodge in Shelbyville, Illinois, loaned out both a 2005 Dodge Daytona Ram and 2006 Charger Daytona for a photo session on a crisp fall day when the local foliage matched the color of the vehicles. Beautiful day, beautiful Dodges. And speaking of Mopars, John Gastman opened the doors to his Roanoke Motor Company in Roanoke, Illinois, and allowed me to leave his lot with a 2005 SRT-10 Commemorative Edition, 2006 SRT-10 Quad Cab, and 2006 Viper for a day's worth of photographic fun. Last, but certainly not least, I can't forget Mark Pelafous of Worden-Martin Lincoln-Mercury in Champaign, Illinois. Mark has helped me more than once over the years, and this time he made it possible to photograph a gorgeous 2003 Harley-Davidson F-150. Thanks also go to Pelafous' righthand man in the shop, Dick Adams.

Various other vehicles appearing on these pages came from private sources. In basic order of appearance, they belong to: 1927 Ford Model T, Bill Broughton, Willington, Alabama; 1918 Dodge Screenside, Roy Brister, Sacramento, California; 1918 Chevrolet Model 490, Tom Snivley, Waterville, Ohio; 1953 Ford F-100, Mike Hauser, Metropolis, Illinois; 1955 Chevrolet Bel Air convertible, Bruce and Linda Finley, Lakeland, Florida; 1955 Chevrolet 3100, Ken Craig, Lakeland, Florida; 1956 and 1958 Chevrolet Cameo Carriers (pair), Ralph Peddicord, Westminster, Maryland; 1957 Dodge Sweptside and 1996 Dodge Indy 500 Official Truck, Jim Elser, Marietta, Georgia; 1959 and 1964 Chevrolet El Caminos (pair); Bill Smith, Hershey, Pennsylvania; 1972 Chevrolet Super Cheyenne, Rob Granger, Eustis, Florida; 1973 Ford Explorer, Kerry Haggard, Commerce, Georgia; 1965 Dodge Custom Sport Special, Greg Tomberlin, Brainerd, Minnesota; 1946 Chevrolet and 1990 Chevrolet 454 SS, Jim Semon, Westlake, Ohio; 1957 Ford Ranchero, Ron Fisher, Indianapolis, Indiana; 1959 Chevrolet El Camino, Doug Stapleton, Bradenton, Florida; 1960 Ford Ranchero, R. Howard Baker, Charlotte, North Carolina; 1965 Chevrolet El Camino, Bill Worthington, Apopka, Florida; 1965 Chevrolet Chevelle SS convertible, Charlie Stinson, Mt. Dora, Florida; 1970 Chevrolet El Camino SS 396, Carl Beck, Clearwater, Florida; 1970 Chevrolet SS 454 El Camino, Robert Inhoff, Jeanette, Pennsylvania; 1970 Chevrolet LS6 454 V8, Jim Lerum, Crystal Lake, Illinois; 1970 Ford 428 Cobra Jet V8, Bill Sneathen, Cape Girardeau, Missouri; 1979 Ford Ranchero, Gene Mackrancy, Port Vue, Pennsylvania; 1981 Chevrolet El Camino Royal Knight, Daryl Miller, Normal, Illinois; 1991 GMC Syclone, Lee Dykes, West Columbia, South Carolina; 2006 Chevrolet Intimidator SS, Bill Anderson, Rantoul, Illinois; 2006 Chevrolet SSR, John Thornton, Lithia Springs, Georgia; 1978 Dodge Li'l Red Truck and 1990 Dodge Li'l Red Dakota, Ken and Carol Merten, St. Cloud, Minnesota; 2004 Dodge Rumble Bee, Chris Lafever, Bloomington, Illinois; 2004 Dodge Hemi GTX, Michael Waller, Champaign, Illinois.

Many thanks to all of you.

When Dodge's vicious Viper debuted for 1990, it featured a V-10 powerplant borrowed from the division's truck lineup. It was then only a matter of time before this hopped-up mill, originally rated at 400 horsepower, made its way back home beneath pickup hoods. In 2004 Dodge introduced its awesome Viper-powered SRT-10 truck, which now claimed 500 horses—more than enough to allow it to also claim the title of world's fastest pickup. At left is a 2006 Viper; at right is a 2005 Commemorative Edition SRT-10.

INTRODUCTION: *Pickin' Up The Pace*

We Americans are so incredibly spoiled in so many different ways. We not only expect a chicken in every pot (proverbial or not), we also take for granted a cell phone in every hand, 800 digital TV channels in every room, and hot- and cold-running e-mail at every turn. Two vehicles out in the garage? Hell, that's been a given for more than a generation or so—with one major twist.

Hit the ever-present electronic opener on today's garage doors and you're likely to find two trucks parked in place of the sedan and station wagon once commonly seen in driveways dating back to the dawn of suburbia. Thanks to the emergence of the minivan and modern Sport Utility Vehicle—coupled with the good ol' pick-'em-up truck's transformation into a kinder, gentler all-purpose machine—the once-traditional automobile has reached superfluous status in many circles, especially those traveled by the scourge of the rapidly fading two-door coupe: the dreaded soccer mom. It's certainly no

Ford kicked off the Big Three truck race in 1917 with its Model TT one-ton, which was sold in bare-chassis form only. America's first steel-bodied, factory complete half-ton pickup, based on the Model T roadster, then followed from Ford in 1925. Shown here is a 1927 Model T truck.

secret that today's families value loads of utility along with heaping helpings of comfort, convenience and class, and Detroit's latest, greatest light trucks cover all those bases like no car ever has. Or ever will.

Funny thing, though: it doesn't seem all that long ago that trucks were trucks, cars were cars, and that was that. Baby-boomers back in the Sixties and Seventies couldn't have envisioned a valet parking area full of utility vehicles, and their parents undoubtedly never imagined seeing light trucks come far off the farm, construction site or such. A pickup's life then was all work, no play. Sure, as far back as the Fifties, some of these broad-shoul-

dered beasts of burden did start taking on some of the comforts of home previously reserved for the car-buying crowd. But as late as the Eighties they still were relegated primarily to the blue-collar world. By the time the new millennium arrived, however, next to no one (wearing a white shirt and tie or not) was thinking twice about the pickup's proper place in polite society.

Prestige and pizzazz are prime selling points nowadays as many Americans expect their trucks to look and act every bit as cool as their fancy-schmancy automotive counterparts. And some buyers even prefer their pickups to perform as well as, or even better than, Detroit's lat-

Dodge's first truck, introduced late in 1917 as a
1918 model, was techni-
cally a commercial car. It
was called a "Screenside"
for rather obvious reasons—
those wire screens in back
hopefully prevented goods
from "walking off" before
a sale could be made. A
true pickup from the Dodge
Brothers' firm was a few
years down the road, as was
an eventual merger with
Walter Chrysler's burgeon-
ing conglomerate. Dodge
became a division of Chrysler in 1928.

est, greatest muscle cars, demonstrating just how much
of the aging fence between the two formerly segregated
vehicle lines has fallen down. For these fast-thinking
customers, the Big Three have rolled out various hot rod
haulers in recent years, with the most prominent being
Dodge's 500-horsepower SRT-10, introduced for 2004.
Powered by the Viper's venomous V-10, this screamer is
now recognized by *The Guinness Book of World Records*
as the "World's Fastest Production Pickup Truck" after
running 150+ mph in February 2004.

That title previously belonged to Ford's supercharged
SVT Lightning, which managed a 147.7 mph top-end
burst in August 2003 to slap down a gauntlet that the

Dodge boys were more than happy to accept. Chevrolet
truck people, too, have been no strangers to the performance pickup race in recent years. Their 345-horse-
power, all-wheel-drive Silverado SS appeared in 2003,
and Chevy's "retro-rod," the retractable-roofed SSR, was
treated to a 390-horse Corvette V-8 two years later.

When and why in the world did this wild race get
started? Perhaps we need to begin at the very beginning.

The Big Three truck legacy itself dates back to 1917,
when Ford rolled out its Model TT one-ton, a bare-
chassis offering that featured a lengthened, reinforced
Model T passenger-car frame fitted with heavy-duty
suspension components. Adding a cab and cargo box

was the customer's responsibility, but that was no problem considering the great number of aftermarket firms then in the business of manufacturing just such items for just such applications.

Dodge's first "truck" (it was actually labeled a "commercial car") appeared late in 1917 with a full body, not just a heavy-duty bare chassis. It had a roof over its cargo bed and wire screens on both sides to help keep the goods in back from "walking off" before the sale could be made. Thus its name: screenside.

Chevrolet also began producing trucks late in 1917. But the Bow-Tie crew did their Blue Oval counterparts one better by introducing two models, both in bare-chassis form: the one-ton Model T and the half-ton Model 490. Again, cabs and beds came by way of the aftermarket. It was left up to Henry Ford's men to finally end this practice and take credit for creating the true American pickup truck.

Introduced for 1925, Fords "Model T Runabout with Pick-Up Body" was not much more than a Model T roadster with a small cargo box mounted in place of the car's rear deck. Nonetheless this combination is widely recognized as being this country's first pickup. Although light-duty pickups had existed before 1925, not one was factory-built—once more, it was the aftermarket that then supplied custom pickup bodies, nearly all made from wood. Ford's Model T half-ton truck broke ground because it was sold complete from the factory with a steel body. No more middlemen suppliers were needed.

Another "factory-complete" pickup, this one from Dodge Brothers, had actually appeared the year before, but it apparently failed to qualify for milestone status due to various technicalities. This 3/4-ton truck featured a wooden body supplied by the Graham Brothers firm, Dodge's Indiana-based "truck division," and it was barely noticed by the truck-buying public. Only about 500 were built in 1924, compared to the 30,000 Model T pickups sold in 1925.

By 1930 both Chevrolet and Dodge (now a division of Chrysler Corporation) were turning out steel-bodied,

Chevrolet introduced two trucks in 1918, the one-ton Model T and half-ton Model 490 (shown here), the latter being based on the division's 490-series automobile. Power for the 1918 Model 490 pickup came from a 26-horsepower, 170 cubic-inch, overhead-valve four-cylinder.

factory-complete half-tons. Chevy's "Cast Iron Wonder," with the division's historic overhead-valve six-cylinder engine, had debuted the year before to help steal away Ford's early lead atop the truck market's sales rankings, kicking off a battle fought tooth and nail for decades to come. Dearborn managed to regain that lead in the early Thirties, but Chevrolet quickly jumped back on top in 1933 and continued leading the way every year up into the Seventies—always with its age-old rival hot on its heels. Today it's Ford folks bragging of a similar winning streak after 30 straight years of building America's best-selling trucks.

Chevrolet got the postwar pickup market rolling with its all-new Advance Design models in 1947. Ford then followed with the first of its long-running F-series trucks in 1948. But before Chevy could reply, the Dearborn crew came right back with Detroit's next thoroughly modern light truck, the F-100, in 1953. The F-100 raised the bar in the utility field as far as comfort and convenience were concerned.

Often overshadowed in decades past, Dodge trucks have always hung in there even while occasionally falling to fourth or fifth place in market rankings, far behind Chevy and Ford, and just aft of GMC and International-Harvester. Fortunately the Dodge Boys no longer have to worry about International, which quit the light-truck game in 1980. Nor were they ever in danger of complete collapse like Studebaker. Dodge's perseverance in the truck market finally paid off in the Nineties when it rose up again into the limelight with an entirely new breed of Ram-tough pickup, a head-turning hauler that reportedly helped change all the rules.

Like International and Studebaker, various other "independents" have come and gone in the truck field over the years, but the market leaders rarely took note dating back to the American pickup's earliest days. As an example, more than half of the 600,000 trucks (of all sizes) built in 1937 came from Chevrolet, Ford and Dodge.

Most of these were pickups, and most were from number one Chevy and number two Ford. As usual, Dodge stood a distant third.

Pickup popularity was on the rise right up until World War II interrupted production of civilian vehicles, and when peace came in 1945 nearly all American truck builders stood poised to supply a hungry market with all-new light-duty trucks. Chevrolet, Ford, Dodge, Studebaker, and International each rolled out thoroughly modern pickups during the late Forties, with Chevy's Advance Design models debuting in 1947 and Ford's fabled F-series the following year. While it didn't make as many headlines as rival rides, Dodge's "Pilot House" model also appeared in 1948. All of these updated vehicles offered the latest in driver comfort and user ease thanks to, among other things, wider cabs, softer seating and enlarged windshields. Exterior styling was also given more attention than ever before.

Enhancing convenience, comfort and class represented the first small steps towards the development of the modern utility vehicle that half of America's drivers depend on for daily transportation today. And in many minds, one giant leap towards this end came in 1953 when Ford introduced its F-100, a light truck milestone if there ever was one.

"Every comfortable, driver-friendly pickup on the road today owes its existence to the original F-100," wrote *Automobile*'s David E. Davis, Jr., in 1996. Davis included the '53 F-100 among his "24 Most Important Automobiles of the Century" because it "was the first truck planned, styled, and engineered by a corporate management team." With the new-and-improved F-100 setting the pace, he added, "suddenly pickup trucks became an alternative for personal transportation."

Not to be outdone, Chevrolet wasted little time following Ford's lead, introducing its gorgeous Task Force trucks two years later. Chevy began the 1955 run with the same light truck it had offered in 1954, a slightly upgraded Advance Design model with a new grille and a one-piece, slightly curved windshield. Then on March 25, General Motors' price leader announced the arrival of its so-called "second-series" 1955 pickup, a high-class half-ton that easily turned heads with its newfound style and flair.

Overall impressions were quite car-like, thanks in part to the deletion of two traditional design features: exposed running boards and pontoon front fenders. The Task Force body's smooth, rounded corners, hooded headlights and "eggcrate" grille were unabashed knock-offs from Chevrolet's equally new 1955 Bel Air. Additional family ties included optional full-wheel covers and a trendy wraparound Panoramic windshield. Panoramic rear glass was available, too.

On its own, Chevrolet's second-series 1955 pickup ranked as Detroit's slickest yet, and its appeal was enhanced further with the addition of seemingly countless options, including Chevy's new overhead-valve small-block V-8. But that wasn't all. New as well that year was a special pickup that stands as the first Ameri-

Chevrolet one-upped Ford's F-100 with its new Task Force line, introduced in March 1955. Styling was now truly a priority for pickup designers. Notice the family ties between Chevy's sensational 1955 Bel Air (left) and its equally new 1955 3100-series half-ton (right).

can utility vehicle to combine real prestige with proven practicality.

Able to both play as well as work, Chevy's 1955 Cameo Carrier stunned truck watchers with its unprecedented stylish flair. Behind its already attractive Task Force cab was a "fleetside" cargo box sheathed in fiberglass panels that did away with those obsolete rear pontoons. Attractive trim adorned those stylish panels allowing for a two-tone paint scheme featuring only one combination: Bombay Ivory and Cardinal Red. In back were car-style taillights.

Though somewhat limited in scope (would you want to risk damaging that beautiful bed by putting this baby

Also introduced in March 1955 was Chevrolet's classy Cameo Carrier, America's first prestigious pickup. All truck up front, the Cameo featured a stylish cargo box done in fiberglass. This beautiful breed ran from 1955 to 1958; at left is a 1958 model, in back at right is a 1956. All 1955 Cameos were painted white. Additional colors debuted the following year.

to work on a farm?), the Cameo was reasonably successful: 5,220 were sold that first year, and production continued up through 1958 (GMC also marketed its own rendition until 1959). On top of that, the Cameo's appearance also inspired a copycat, Dodge's Sweptside, which featured station wagon rear quarter panels in back complete with Chrysler Corporation's trademark soaring tail fins. Nowhere near as popular as the Cameo, the somewhat odd Sweptside was built in lesser numbers from 1957 to 1959.

Two years after Chevrolet first demonstrated that the car and truck worlds didn't have to be polar opposites, Ford came up with what product planners today might as well call the industry's first "crossover," the 1957 Ranchero. Mostly car, partly truck, the Ranchero not only survived on the market until 1979, it also inspired its own copy, Chevy's El Camino, produced from 1959 to 1988. During those years each of these car-truck combos came in high-performance versions, variants built

by simply borrowing hot parts from the automotive models they were based on.

As the Sixties dawned it was clear that the times certainly were a-changin' in the truck market. Options like power steering and brakes, air conditioning and V-8 muscle were growing in popularity, as were pickups themselves. Total truck sales in American hovered around the one million mark in 1960, making up 12.5 percent of the vehicle market. Sales surpassed two million in 1971, and the market share hit 20 percent the following year. Almost lost during this numbers surge was Dodge's introduction of this country's first muscle truck, the 1964 Custom Sports Special, powered optionally by the company's 426 cubic-inch wedge-head V-8.

Although no direct response to the Custom Sports Special appeared from Chevrolet and Ford, there were various sporty models introduced during the Seventies, including the former's Cheyenne and the latter's Explorer, nicely tricked-out trucks with humble doses of pres-

Dodge followed up Chevrolet's Cameo with its Sweptside (right) in 1957, a half-ton hauler that incorporated station wagon quarter-panels in back. Nearly forty years later, another flashy Dodge truck arrived, this one commemorating the Viper's appearance as the prestigious pace car for the 1996 Indianapolis 500. This Indy 500 Special Edition Ram was painted to match the Viper GTS coupe pace car.

tige. Another true muscle-bound pickup didn't appear until Dodge tried this adventurous niche again with its Li'l Red Truck in 1978. Dodge's definitely hot half-ton proved to be somewhat of a sensation at a time when the great American muscle car was all but dead, yet the performance pickup concept still couldn't quite catch on. Nothing comparable was developed during the Eighties.

The Nineties, however, were a different story, undoubtedly due to the pickup's upwardly advancing ac-

ceptance in the mainstream. Chevrolet's SS 454 C1500, GMC's Syclone and Ford's SVT Lightning all made big splashes during this decade, and there's been no shortage of power in the pickup field since. Even GM's latest luxury loadmaster, Cadillac's Escalade EXT, now can brag of 403 horses as these words go to print in 2007.

Such glorious prestige and power all wrapped up in a pickup body—only in America, land of the free and home of the spoiled.

Ford kicked off the modern half-car/half-truck era in 1957 with its Ranchero. Chevrolet then followed suit with its El Camino in 1959 (right). Dearborn designers then downsized their hybrid in 1960, as did Chevrolet, to a much lesser degree in 1964 (left). The Chevelle-based El Camino proved to be the perfect platform as far as performance-oriented pickups were concerned.

Comfort and convenience options like air conditioning and automatic transmissions began gaining ground in pickup ranks during the Sixties, as did classy appearance packages later in the decade. In 1967, Chevrolet introduced its Custom Sport Truck package, which added extra trim outside and flashy appointments inside. Even cooler was Chevy's Cheyenne, first seen in 1971. A dressier Super Cheyenne package (shown here) was unveiled in 1972.

Ford's highest-class haulers for the Seventies were called Explorers. Special trim, bed rails, side mirrors and exclusive paint—in this 1973 Explorer's case, Grabber Blue borrowed from the Mustang palate—were just part of the attraction.

Dodge deserves credit for building Detroit's first muscle truck, the Custom Sport Special, introduced for 1964. Twin racing stripes and bucket seats were standard. Optional power came from a 365-horsepowe, 426 cubic-inch wedge-head V-8. Shown here is a 1965 model.

What a difference forty-something years can make. When peacetime pickup production got rolling again after World War II, Chevrolet simply picked up where it had left off before World War II—its 1946 model (right) was more or less a pre-war leftover that remained all work, no play. By the time the 454 SS appeared for 1990 (left), light trucks had morphed into big boys' toys.

Pickups have been running on drag strips dating back to the sport's earliest days, but were always few and far between to say the least. Finally, in 1998, the National Hot Rod Association (NHRA) announced its Pro Stock Truck division. Back in the Sixties the most prominent drag trucks were exhibition vehicles, like Bill Golden's "Little Red Wagon." This crowd-pleasing, Hemi-powered A-100 Dodge did its first wheelstand in 1964. Today it resides in Don Garlits' Museum of Drag Racing outside Ocala, Florida.

Pickups first took to NASCAR tracks on an exhibition basis in 1994. Then the Craftsman Truck Series officially opened for business in 1995. Mike Skinner's familiar #3 Chevrolet took that first seasonal championship, and Chevys won fifty of the tour's first seventy races.

Before Dodge's SRT-10 became the world's fastest pickup, that honor belonged to Ford's Lightning, a product of the company's Special Vehicle Team performance wing. Introduced for 1993, the first-generation Lightning pickup was powered by a 240-horsepower, 351 cubic-inch V-8. A supercharged 5.4-liter V-8 appeared along with the second-generation Lightning in 1999. The 2001 Lightning (shown here) featured 380 blown horses.

Though by no means a muscle truck, Lincoln's 2002 Blackwood certainly qualified as a big boy's toy—a well-to-do big boy, that is. This country club cruiser cost about $52,000. Beneath the hood was a 300-horsepower 5.4-liter V8.

Dodge rolled out its Ram Daytona pickup in 2005, then followed that up with a Charger Daytona R/T in 2006. Both appear here in "Go Man Go" paint. Both also feature Hemi power.

Today's top-shelf trucks go where no pickups have gone before—witness the 2007 Cadillac Escalade EXT, a luxurious half-ton hauler with 403 horsepower.

Ford designers created the Ranchero by basically cutting the rear roof section off a 1957 station wagon. Public introduction came in November 1956 in Quitman, Georgia.

Chapter One
HALF BREEDS:
Ford's Ranchero and Chevrolet's El Camino

Why build muscle trucks? Why not? With so much car-style pizzazz and prestige finding its way into the pickup world during recent decades, it was only natural that performance too would make a similar defection. Plain and simply put, Detroit's latest, greatest high-performance haulers owe their existence to the blurring of the line between passenger car and pickup, a slow but sure evolution that dates back nearly sixty years. Still looking quite boldfaced prior to 1950, that demarcation began dimming soon afterwards, with much of the early erasing coming in 1955 when Chevrolet announced its

lovely Cameo Carrier, a truck that carried considerable car-like style and flair in back. The Cameo was no hot rod, mind you, even with Chevy's new milestone, its 265 cubic-inch small-block V-8, bolted in up front. But it was so damned cool, something no other utility vehicle before could come close to claiming. And it also inspired the production of an intriguing breed of "pickup" that would foster various high-powered offspring during its long run.

Unlike Dodge, Ford's better idea people responded to the Cameo not by dressing up a truck like a car, choos-

All options available to Ford passenger-car customers in 1957 carried over into Ranchero ranks, including the rare supercharged 312 cubic-inch V-8.

ing instead the opposite tack. Introduced in November 1956, the truly new Ranchero was touted by Dearborn's promotional people as "America's first work or play truck" somewhat of a misnomer considering this vehicle was more or less simply a station wagon with its rear roof area removed to expose a cargo box. Dearborn officials themselves weren't all that sure of what they had that first year. Their plan basically involved rolling the Ranchero out with high hopes that an ample market would develop overnight for such an unproven product.

That it did, and two year later Chevrolet certified things with a copycat counter-response, the El Camino, also created by stripping off part of a station wagon's roof. From there longevity told the tale. Ford's Ranchero reappeared annually on the American automotive scene for 23 years, while its competitor survived through 27 model runs, but not consecutively. Temporarily shelved after 1960, Chevrolet's El Camino reappeared in 1964 and rolled on up through early 1988. Dearborn's product planners, meanwhile, recognized the end to a long, well-traveled trail a bit earlier, closing the tailgate on their Ranchero line in 1979.

Both rivals experienced a transformation or two during their long, storied careers. In 1960 the Ranchero was reintroduced as a variation on Ford's all-new compact Falcon theme, a petite roll it played reasonably well up through 1966. Ranchero then became a Fairlane offering in 1967 as it jumped up a notch into Dearborn's intermediate ranks, where it would stay through evolutions as a Torino-based model (until 1977) followed by an LTD II variation for its last three renditions.

Like Ranchero, Chevrolet's hybrid half-ton too was born again in downsized form in the early Sixties, only not so small. For 1964, Chevy introduced its mid-sized Chevelle, and this A-body platform was used as a base for a second-generation El Camino, a sporty utility vehicle that quickly soared in popularity, outselling its rival from Ford by at least a two-to-one margin almost every year.

A GMC version of the El Camino, the Sprint, debuted in 1971, then was superseded by the repackaged Caballero in 1978. Like the El Camino, GMC's Caballero carried on, in considerably smaller counts, until 1988.

Chevy's El Camino was introduced to the public in October 1958. Like the Ranchero, this utility vehicle also could've been fitted with any option available in the company's passenger-car ranks that year. This '59 El Camino is powered by the fabled 409 V-8's forerunner, the 348 cubic-inch V-8.

As for total numbers, the copy easily stole the show from the original. Including 36,576 Sprints and 37,719 Caballeros from GMC, all-time El Camino production surpassed one million by 56,424 units. Ford sold 508,355 Rancheros from 1957 to '79: 45,814 first-generation versions, 139,694 Falcon-based models, and 322,847 of the rest. Peak year for both Ford and Chevrolet was 1973, with 45,741 Rancheros and 64,987 El Caminos reaching circulation, joined by 6,7766 GMC Sprints—also a high for that particular package. GMC's actual zenith came in 1979 when 6,952 Caballeros were built. That same year, El Camino production hit its second highest total, 58,008 units, all this coming while Ford men were watching their last Ranchero roll out the door.

During those years both rivals represented various different machines for various different drivers. Being cars, they could've been fitted with nearly every feature found in automotive ranks—flashy paint and trim packages, air conditioning, power assists, you name it. Passenger car performance options too were fair game; right off the bat in 1957 it was entirely possible—albeit briefly—to equip Ford's first Ranchero with either of the two top Thunderbird 312 V-8s, one crowned with twin four-barrel carburetors, the other force-fed by a McCulloch supercharger. Output ratings were 300 horsepower for the latter, 270 for the former.

Leading the way beneath the original El Camino's hood was Chevrolet's optional 348 cubic-inch "W-head" V-8, the fearsome forerunner to the division's famed 409. Offered in passenger-car ranks from 1958 to '61, the 348 was meant to run hot in all applications. All varieties featured high compression (9.5:1 or better), all relied on at least a four-barrel carburetor (no single two-barrels; no way, no how), and all belched out through

Offered from 1958 to 1961 in Chevrolet passenger-cars, the 348 V-8 was a high-performance powerplant that came standard with dual exhausts and nothing short of a four-barrel carburetor—no wimpy two-barrels here. At the top of the 348 lineup was the optional triple-carb version, which produced as many as 335 horses in 1959.

dual exhausts. The ultimate 348 available during its four-year run was the Super Turbo-Thrust, which was fed by three Rochester two-barrels and used solid-lifters in place of the tamer Turbo-Thrust's hydraulic units.

Four different 348s were initially advertised in 1959. Two four-barrel Turbo-Thrust V-8s—one with 9.5:1 compression, the other with 11:1—were listed. Ratings were 250 and 300 horsepower, respectively. Two triple-carb Super Turbo-Thrusts, they too with either 9.5:1 or 11:1 compression, were also listed. Output ratings for these two beasts were 280 and 315 horses.

About midyear Chevy engineers traded the 315-horse Super Turbo-Thrust 348 for the even more powerful 335-horsepower Special Super Turbo-Thrust, which featured streamlined exhaust manifolds and 11.25:1 compression. Some sources rated this engine at 345 horsepower, and others list 305- and 320-horse ratings, numbers that were advertised prominently on the hoods of NASCAR stock cars in 1959. More confusion was

created when engineers added better heads with bigger ports and valves, creating the 350-horsepower Special Super Turbo-Thrust 348 for 1960. Some reports claim this high-strung, high-powered factory race engine first appeared late in 1959. Whatever the rating, adding any of the 348 W-heads into the El Camino equation in 1959 and '60 resulted in a utility vehicle that was, in *Motor Life's* words, "almost too potent for normal driving."

Most El Camino buyers, however, never experienced such a rush as the main appeal was this machine's polite practicality—348-equipped models were rare to say the least. Including all engines, sixes or V-8s, El Camino production for 1959 was 22,246, half again more than Ford's total for its last full-sized Ranchero. Sales then lagged by fifty percent the next year before the lineage went on hiatus.

Dropping down into Chevrolet's newborn mid-sized ranks proved to be just the ticket for the El Camino: 36,615 were sold in 1964—more than twice the num-

Ford reinvented its Ranchero on the compact Falcon platform in 1960. Ranchero and El Camino wouldn't meet again on the same playing field until 1967.

ber of Falcon Rancheros Ford moved that year. From there, the attraction continued growing as more sporty impressions began filtering into the mix.

Like the Chevelle, the El Camino could've been fitted with a host of hot small-block V-8s in 1964, right up to the Corvette's 350-horse L79 327. And by 1966, almost everything the Chevelle SS offered to muscle car buyers, including the definitely hot 396-cid Mk IV big-block V-8 (rated as high as 375 horsepower), had become an El Camino option. Exceptions included the popular Super Sport nomenclature itself. In 1966 and '67 the Mk IV big-block was only available in Chevelle ranks as part of the SS 396 performance package. El Camino buyers could order the 396—as well as bucket seats, a console and the SS 396's mag-style wheel covers—but they couldn't get all that snazzy SS imagery.

The situation finally changed in 1968 when Chevrolet introduced its honest-to-goodness SS 396 El Camino, complete with those revered "SS 396" badges, an attractive blacked-out grille and a special hood adorned with parallel "power bulges." "Fancier than a truck, more utilitarian than a passenger car, able to leap past sports cars in a single bound, the [SS 396] El Camino will fill needs that the owner never knew he had." Or so claimed a *Car Life* report, which posted an impressive quarter-mile time of 14.80 seconds for the latest member of Chevy's hot-to-trot Super Sport fraternity. According to *Hot Rod* magazine's Steve Kelley, the '68 SS 396 El Camino was "the near-perfect 'Gentleman's hauler.'"

New for 1969 was the way Chevrolet marketed its mid-sized Super Sports. While the two SS 396 cousins,

Chevrolet dropped its El Camino after 1960, then returned with a mid-sized rendition based on the new mid-sized Chevelle in 1964. Again the El Camino benefited from its car-line roots as Chevelle engine options carried over with no fuss or muss. The 1965 El Camino shown in front here features a hot-to-trot 350-horsepower 327 cubic-inch V-8. In back is a 283-powered 1965 Chevelle SS convertible.

Chevelle and El Camino, were listed as individual models in 1968, all that SS stuff was repackaged as an options group, labeled RPO Z25, in 1969. Included in the Z25 deal was a 325-horse 396, a beefier chassis, the familiar SS 396 dress-up, new 14x7 five-spoke SS wheels, and power front disc brakes.

Even more repackaging came in 1970 as the tried-and-true SS 396 was joined by its SS 454 big brother. Ordering this supreme Super Sport required checking off RPO Z15. The Z25 and Z15 groups were basically identical save for the obvious exchange of the former's

396 V-8 (now rated at 350 horsepower) for the latter's LS5 454-cube Mk IV big-block, rated at 360 horses.

A second 454, the famed LS6, also could've been added into the Z15 deal in 1970, though few El Camino buyers opted for this outrageous big-block, considered by many to be the meanest mill unleashed during the muscle car era. Output was a whopping 450 horses, a figure that some witnesses still claim was on the conservative side.

Chevrolet's promotion of the El Camino as a sporty plaything typically inspired a similar effort at Ford,

The Chevelle-based El Camino looked great from any angle, and could work every bit as hard as it played.

which in 1967 began helping Ranchero customers forget all about those small-thinking Falcon years. Newfound prestige came along by way of the dressier mid-sized Fairlane Ranchero 500 and even more upscale Fairlane Ranchero 500 XL, the latter fitted with a sporty bucket seat/console interior. Top optional oomph came from a 315-horsepower 390 cubic-inch big-block V-8.

Ford dropped the Fairlane reference in 1968. And with Chevy's SS 396 El Camino running about, Dearborn also traded its topline XL model for a real sport truck, the Ranchero GT. GT imagery included appropriate badges, special striping and styled-steel wheels with "GT" center caps. A 390 V-8, this one rated at 325 horses, was again the top choice under a Ranchero's hood.

By 1968 it had become obvious that work had given way to play in the car/truck field. "El Camino and Ranchero have established a new trend in the fun car market, and people all over the country are getting on the bandwagon," claimed *Motorcade* magazine's Lee Kelley in a December 1967 report. Ford's efforts to keep up with Chevrolet in the fun market included adding the 335-horse 428 Cobra Jet V-8 to the Ranchero's options list for 1969. Adding the optional ram-air Cobra Jet also brought along a functional hood scoop to further enhance the Ranchero's performance image.

That add-on hood scoop was replaced with Ford's unforgettable "Shaker" when a ram-air engine was ordered in 1970. This sexy scoop protruded right through an opening in the hood, vibrating along with the V-8 below whenever the throttle was blipped, hence its name. Serving up the most shakes beneath 1970 Ranchero GT hoods was Ford's equally new 429 cubic-inch Cobra Jet V-8, rated at 370 horsepower. Like so many other muscle car mills, the 429 CJ was cancelled after 1971, in this case leaving the 351 Cleveland small-block V-8 as the Ranchero's hottest power source.

As high-performance began fading away in the Seventies, Ford and Chevrolet started trading horsepower for dress-up imagery to help turn customers' heads. Two-

The 350-horse 327 V-8, option code L79, was introduced for the Corvette in 1965 and also trickled down into the Chevelle that year. Compression was 11:1

tone paint schemes and tape stripes abounded for both Ranchero and El Camino, and sporty GT and SS renditions were offered right up to the end. Lesser known appearance options included the El Camino's Conquista paint package, available from 1974 to '77, and in 1978 Chevrolet and GMC began offering special-edition black-only models—Royal Knight and Diablo, respectively—each featuring a large, Trans Am–like hood decal. Then Dearborn marked the end of the Ranchero line in 1979 with a Limited Production version, a truly dressy concoction that came complete with an exclusive exterior plate engraved with the owner's initials.

Devoted followers still love Ranchero and El Camino for the way they played as hard as they worked.

While many Super Sport pieces could've been ordered on early El Caminos, Chevy's half-car/half-truck didn't officially enter SS ranks until 1968. Like its SS 396 Chevelle running mate, the 1968 SS 396 El Camino came standard with a 325-horsepower, 396 cubic-inch Mk IV big-block V-8. A 1970 SS 396, fitted with a 350-horsepower big-block, appears here.

Like the Chevelle, the El Camino appeared in two Super Sport forms for 1970: SS 396 and SS 454. Total SS 454 production that year, for both Chevelle and El Camino, was 8,773.

Two 454 big-blocks were offered in 1970, beginning with the LS5 rendition (shown here), rated at 360 horsepower. LS5 installations (in both Chevelles and El Caminos) numbered 4,298 in 1970.

Chevrolet's Mk IV V-8 was bored out from 396 cubic inches to 402 late in 1969, but the famed name remained in both Chevelle and El Camino ranks: SS 396. The base SS 396 V-8 went from 325 horsepower to 350 for 1970.

An entirely different animal, the LS6 454 V-8 is considered by many to be the muscle car era's biggest, baddest powerplant. Its output rating, 450 horsepower, was not only Detroit's most impressive to date, it was no lie. Although much more expensive than its LS5 brother, the LS6 actually outsold the 360-horsepower 454—1970 production was 4,475.

Fortunately the Ranchero gained back some size and prestige as the Sixties rolled on. It became a mid-sized Fairlane model in 1967. And by 1971 it was looking every bit as snazzy as its El Camino rival. Ford's 1971 utility lineup appears here, with a Ranchero GT representing the star of the show.

Introduced in April 1968, Ford's 428 Cobra Jet V-8 was every bit a match for Chevrolet's 396. Conservatively rate at 335 horsepower, it eventually found its way beneath Ranchero hoods. In 1970 it was superseded by Ford's 429 Cobra Jet V-8, which produced 370 horsepower.

The Ranchero legacy came to an end in 1979. This dressy Limited Edition model served as a suitable send-off for the long-running breed.

El Camino production continued on into early 1988 before ceasing. Snazzy models during those last years included the Royal Knight, introduced in 1981.

This hood treatment was standard for the 1981 Royal Knight El Camino.

Four-speeds were rare by 1981, but this Royal Knight was originally ordered with one.

Chevrolet's proud Super Sport legacy, initiated in 1961, entered into its truck phase in 1990. Done in monochromatic black, the 454 SS half-ton pickup rolled on 15x7 chrome wheels and featured a sport suspension.

Chapter Two
SIMPLY SUPER:
Sizzling Chevrolets (and one GMC)

Chevrolet's seemingly ageless SS image has shown up on everything from compacts to full-sized four-doors over the years, dating back to the original too-cool-for-school Super Sport, which debuted in the Impala line in 1961. The diminutive Nova SS followed in 1963, the intermediate Chevelle SS appeared the following year, the Mustang-inspired Camaro SS made the scene in 1967, and the dual-purpose El Camino SS joined the fraternity in 1968. In 1970 Chevy's new Monte Carlo too took on Super Sport guise, coupling that soft-spoken SS pizzazz with some serious performance supplied by the division's beastly 454 cubic-inch Mk IV big-block V-8.

Introduced at 396 cubic inches in 1965, the Mk IV V-8 was boosted to 427 cubes the following year, then to a whopping 454 in 1970. Top output was 450 horsepower from the fabled LS6 big-block, offered as an SS 454 Chevelle/El Camino option for 1970 only. In 1971 the LS6 was limited to Corvette applications, where it was slightly detuned to 425 horses. Lesser 454 renditions followed from there as tightening federal emissions standards quickly brought Detroit's original muscle car era to an abrupt end.

The heart of the 454 SS was Chevy's long-running Mk IV V-8, born in 1965. As the name implied, this big-block displaced 454 cubic inches. Output was 230 horsepower in 1990. It went up to 255 horses for the 1991 454 SS.

The 454 then made it back into the limelight as Chevrolet kicked off America's modern muscle truck race in 1990. After warming things up in the pickup field with its Li'l Red Truck in 1978, Dodge had retreated during the Eighties, relying more on sporty appearance packages, including a short run of convertible Dakota mini-trucks beginning in 1989. A limited collection (1,500 built) of V-8-powered Shelby Dakota pickups also appeared that year, but that was pretty much the limit as far as real performance was concerned during a decade that basically left lead-foots tapping their toes in quiet desperation. Then along came Chevrolet's 454 SS C-1500 half-ton to further establish the pickup's rightful place on the big boys' playground.

Standing tall as the meanest muscle truck to date,

Chevy's 1990 454 SS looked especially bad all done up in black with an air dam hugging the road up front and special 15x7 chromed wheels complementing things at the corners. Sticky P275/60HR tires adorned those rims, and the suspension was further tweaked with Bilstein gas-charged shocks, a thickened front stabilizer bar, and quickened steering gear. High-back bucket seats were standard inside, but the main attraction came behind this sinister short-bed's blacked-out grille—as the name implied, the 454 SS was powered by the venerable Mk IV big-block, now listed as a 7.4-liter V-8 to appease the metric-minded gods. Output was a net-rated 230 horsepower, nothing to sneeze at a quarter century ago.

Though slow sellers at first, the pricey (around $20,000), fully loaded 454 SS did develop a humble

High-back bucket seats were standard inside the 1990 454 SS pickup. A 1993 road test put 454 SS performance at 7.1 seconds for the time-honored 0–60 run, 15.7 seconds (at 87 mph) for the quarter-mile

following, allowing it to stay in the scene up through 1993. More power (255 horses) came along in 1991 while the remaining package carried on in familiar fashion. By the time the 454 SS ran its course, Ford had its SVT Lightning up and running, and Dodge was waiting right around the corner with its all-new Ram to serve as a base for some really hot trucks to come. Getting the ball rolling again, rather briskly this time, in the muscle truck field was the short-lived 454 SS Chevy's legacy. It also led the way for another Super Sport pickup, a

reasonably warm compact truck offered in S-10 ranks from 1994 to '98.

Easily the hottest mini-truck ever built came from General Motors in 1991, in this case from the corporation's other truck line, GMC, with a little cooperation from the folks at Production Automotive Services in Troy, Michigan. Using GMC's compact Sonoma as a base, the PAS people huffed and puffed and blew the doors off any and all performance pickups then on the road with the aptly named Syclone, phonetically spelled

The quickest vehicle Detroit offered in 1991 wasn't a car; it was GMC's little Syclone, a custom-built Sonoma fitted with a turbocharged six-cylinder and all-wheel drive. Production was only 2,995 in 1991, all painted black, save for 10 re-painted red models created as promotional pieces for Marlboro cigarettes. Apparently three more Syclones were built in 1992 before this hell-raising hauler rolled off into the history books.

because Mercury still held rights to the dictionary-correct Cyclone tag.

Size in this case clearly didn't matter, nor did classification. Many muscle cars then running around were no match for the little Syclone, which could blast through the quarter-mile in a mere 14.1 seconds. Rest to 60 mph went by in 5.3 quick ticks. Such sensational performance was made possible by a turbocharged, intercooled 4.3-liter V-6 rated (some say conservatively) at 280 horsepower. Behind that six was an electronic

four-speed automatic transmission that delivered those ponies to all four wheels via a Borg-Warner transfer case. Four-wheel anti-lock brakes also were standard.

On the topside, the all-wheel-drive Syclone came only in black, complemented with lower body cladding and a tonneau cover out back. Sixteen-inch alloy wheels wearing 245/50VR Firestone Firehawk tires kept things off the ground, while interior appointments included sport bucket seats, a leather-wrapped steering wheel, and a console with floor shifter. Base price was

Mercury already claimed the "Cyclone" name when GMC released its hot rod pickup in 1991; the guys at General Motors' other truck division simply changed the spelling on their all-black stormer. In a *Car and Driver* test, a Syclone outran a Ferrari 348. Posted 0–60 time was 5.3 seconds, 14.1 seconds for the quarter-mile. With a little tweaking, 0–60 runs well into the 4-second bracket were no sweat, as were low 13-second quarter-mile bursts.

The Syclone's intercooled, turbocharged 4.3-liter V-6 was factory rated at 280 horsepower, but some sources claim as many as 330 horses actually worked beneath that black hood. Modifications are common as Syclone owners today continually pursue even greater performance from their rides. Owner Lee Dykes bought this Syclone new and has since transformed it into a beast capable of 10.91 seconds in the quarter-mile. Rest to 60 mph requires only a scant 2.97 seconds.

Appropriately embroidered (with "Syclone" stitching) high-back bucket seats and a console with floor shifter were standard inside GMC's world-beater. The shifter was a Corvette item, while instrumentation came from Pontiac's Sunbird Turbo GT.

$25,500—a bunch for a full-sized half-ton in 1991, a veritable king's ransom for a mini-pickup. GMC offered this high-priced, hotter-than-hell compact for that year only, then followed it up with the similarly equipped Typhoon sport-utility-vehicle in 1992 and 1993. Both models remain prized collector pieces today.

A muscle truck from General Motors didn't come close to posting Syclone-type performance numbers until 2003 when Chevrolet folks dusted off their SS badges yet again, this time sticking them onto the Silverado extended-cab half-ton. Standard power for this super sport truck came from a high-output version of GM's LQ9 Vortec 6000 V-8 that produced 345 horses. A Hyrdra-Matic 4L85-E four-speed automatic overdrive transmission and full-time all-wheel-drive were standard, as was a Z60 high-performance chassis featuring 20-inch wheels (the Silverado's largest to date) shod in P275/55R20 Goodyear Eagles.

According to *Car and Driver*, the 2003 SS could go 0–60 in 6.3 seconds and finish the quarter-mile in 14.8 clicks, both figures representing improvements of nearly one second compared to the 454 SS of ten years before. "For such a big, heavy vehicle, the SS puts up acceleration, braking and handling numbers that are more akin to those in our last V-6 sports-sedan comparison test," wrote *Car and Driver's* Ron Kiino. "Yes, [Ford's] Lightning and [Dodge's] SRT-10 are faster, more legitimately sporting trucks, but the SS offers the space, versatility, and all-season capability the others don't."

Chevrolet product planners opted to trade off that all-season advantage late in 2005, transforming the 345-horse Silverado SS from an all-wheel-drive truck to a conventional rear driver, to the delight of tire salesmen across the land. Unlike previous traction-conscious renditions, the latest SS pickup could melt its rear rubber off the line with the best of 'em, a plain fact not missed by the press. *AutoWeek* called the new rear-drive SS a "Super Smoker."

The 2WD SS rolled on into 2006 and was joined by a special commemorative edition, the Intimidator SS. Announced in April 2005, the Intimidator SS was cre-ated to honor the late NASCAR legend Dale Earnhardt, with a donation made to his charity foundation for each sale of the 1,333 models planned for 2006.

"We are very proud of the long-time association between Chevrolet and the Earnhardt family," said Chevrolet general manager Ed Peper. "Dale's legacy is unique within racing, and we are excited about this opportunity to offer fans a vehicle they can so closely identify with one of their heroes."

Standard features included an expected black monochromatic exterior adorned with "Intimidator" badges on the tailgates and doors, a unique silver insert in the grille, 20-inch chrome wheels, and a NASCAR-inspired spoiler on the tailgate. Ride height was lowered a bit, and a modified suspension incorporated two-stage multi-leaf springs, Tenneco shocks, a stiffened front stabilizer, and beefier front jounce bumpers. Special Earnhardt commemoration also was added inside. Remaining mechanicals were standard Silverado SS.

The 2006 Silverado Intimidator SS was the sixth commemorative model to honor Chevrolet's NASCAR drivers, with the first five being Monte Carlos. The 2002 Dale Earnhardt Signature Edition kicked things off, followed by the 2003 Jeff Gordon Signature Edition, the 2004 Monte Carlo Intimidator SS, the 2004 Dale Earnhardt Jr. Signature Series supercharged SS Monte Carlo, and the 2005 Tony Stewart Signature Series supercharged SS.

Those two familiar letters also showed up on another playtoy pickup from Chevrolet, only this time with a little more of the alphabet along for the ride. Introduced in concept form at the Detroit auto show in January 2000, Chevy's retro-styled SSR represented an entirely new breed in itself. As marketing director Janet Eckhoff explained it in March 2003, "[it's] like nothing else in the market today. It's part roadster, part pickup and is a commonly innovative expression of Chevy's proud heritage." Indeed, "SSR" stands for "Super Sport Roadster." At the press of a button, this truck's retractable roof folds up and stows away between the passenger compartment and cargo box. Cool is simply not a big enough word.

Chevrolet came back with a Super Sport truck in 2003, this time powering it with a 345-horse 6.0-liter Vortec V-8. All-wheel-drive remained standard beneath the Silverado SS into 2004. Conventional rear-wheel-drive appeared for the SS pickup in 2005.

After teasing the Bow-Tie faithful for a while, Chevrolet made its topless truck a production reality in 2003, and everything about it, from its name on down, said free spirit. "The SSR is the latest in a series of SS-branded Chevy cars and trucks that will rekindle the fun-to-drive heritage of the Super Sport name," added Eckhoff.

Chevrolet's first SSR was powered by a 5.3-liter Vortec V-8 with its cylinder block and heads cast of aluminum. Output was 300 horsepower, and the only transmission available was the electronic four-speed Hydra-Matic automatic (w/overdrive). Factory reports claimed performance figures of 7.6 seconds for the 0–60 run and 15.9 (at 90 mph) for the quarter-mile.

For 2005, a new and improved SSR appeared with a more solid platform and more muscle, this time supplied by the new C6 Corvette's 6.0-liter LS2 V-8. Beneath the 2005 Corvette's hood, the LS2 was rated at 400 horsepower; in SSR garb it was tagged at 390 horses. New too for the '05 SSR was an optional Tremec six-speed manual gearbox, joined in back by an Eaton locking differential in a beefed-up 14-bolt rear axle. Automatic models relied on a 12-bolt rear and standard electronic traction control.

According to *Truck Trend*, the six-speed, LS2 SSR could downright get it: 0–60 in 5.58 seconds, 13.95 seconds at 102.2 mph for the quarter-mile. No matter how you slice it, that's simply one super Chevy.

Dale Earnhardt's favored black was the only color available for the monochromatic Intimidator SS in 2006. A silver grille insert complemented things up front.

Chrome 20-inch wheels were standard for the 2006 Intimidator SS, as was a performance suspension that lowered ride height an inch or so. A spoiler brought up the tail.

The Intimidator edition shared the Silverado SS pick-up's 345-horse 6.0-liter Vortec V-8. Torque was 380 lb-ft. Delivering this muscle to the road was a four-speed automatic transmission and 3.73:1 gears out back. Coolers for engine oil and transmission fluid were standard.

The Intimidator SS was the sixth commemorative model released by Chevrolet to honor its NAS-CAR heroes. The first five were Monte Carlos.

Special treatments inside the Intimidator SS included appropriate "Intimidator" identification on the instrument panel and floor mats and an autographed tachometer face.

Headrests on the Intimidator SS's front seats also were embroidered with special Dale Earnhardt Legacy logos.

Introduced at the Detroit auto show in concept vehicle form in January 2000, Chevrolet's sexy SSR pickup went into regular production in 2003. Retro styling was only the beginning. This truck's roof was retractable, making topless driving possible.

The original SSR was powered by a 300-horsepower 5.3-liter Vortec V-8. The only transmission available was a four-speed automatic.

The unmistakable SSR looked equally cool with its top up or down. Standard wheels for the 2006 edition were 19x8 units in front, 20x10 in back. Sizes for the Goodyear rubber were P255/45ZR19 at the nose, P295/40R20 at the tail.

According to *Truck Trend* magazine, a six-speed LS2 SSR could run from rest to 60 mph in a mere 5.58 seconds. The quarter-mile time slip was 13.95 seconds at 102.2 mph.

The SSR's roof folded away behind the cab quickly and rather quietly at the push of a button on the console. Cargo volume beneath that tonneau cover was 22.5 cubic feet.

For 2005, the SSR was treated to chassis refinements and the C6 Corvette's 6.0-liter LS2 V-8. Rated at 400 horse-power in automotive ranks, the LS2 was tagged at 390 horses for the 2005 SSR. An optional six-speed Tremec manual-transmission also appeared this year. For 2006, the six-speed LS2 (shown here) was boosted back up to 400 horsepower, while its automatic trans running mate was re-rated at 395 horses.

Retro touches carried over inside to the SSR's dashboard. Gauges included a torque readout.

Gone with the wind. Like so many other play toys, Chevrolet's SSR pickup was short lived. It retired at the end of 2006.

Ford's Special Vehicle Team rolled out its first Lightning F-150 truck in 1993 along with its first Cobra Mustang. Production in 1993 was 5,276.

Chapter Three
BLOWN AWAY: *Fast F-150 Fords*

Product planners at Chevrolet and Ford never even cast a backward glance when Dodge introduced Detroit's first muscle truck, the Custom Sports Special, in 1964. Nor did they bother to respond in kind when the Mopar gang came back with another performance pickup, the Li'l Red Truck, in 1978. It was a different story, however, after Chevy helped get the Nineties rolling in fast fashion with its 454 SS. This time push led nearly directly to shove.

Dearborn's response arrived in 1993 by way of its Special Vehicle Team, founded in 1991 to (in the company's own words) "use the best-available resources both from within and without Ford to explore new ways of creating and marketing high-performance vehicles for sale in limited numbers." Of those special vehicles, the Mustang Cobra, built from 1993 to 2004, is best remembered, with the SVT Contour (1998–2000) and Focus (2002–2004) models trailing in its shadow. The

The original SVT Lightning was not only quick, it also featured an exceptional (in pickup terms) chassis. Ride height was one inch lower in front, 2.5 inches in back. Standard wheels were 17x8 cast-aluminum units wearing Firestone Firehawk tires.

team also was involved with the exotic Ford GT (2005–2006), and SVT identification still appears on the new 2007 Shelby Cobra GT500 even though the original organization was all but dissolved a year or so ago.

Along with these fun machines, SVT also dabbled in trucks, introducing the F-150 Lightning along with its first Cobra in February 1993. Like the Cobra, the Lightning wasn't just a matter of more motor; much work also went into making it arguably Detroit's best handling half-ton hauler to date. "The net result is a chassis that feels like it belongs under a sports car," claimed a 1993 SVT brochure. "During developmental tests at Ford's Dearborn, Michigan, proving grounds, the Lightning consistently stretched smiles across the faces of some very tough-to-please critics, including Formula One champion Jackie Stewart."

Suspension tweaks began with a lowered center of gravity: one inch in front, 2.5 in back. Thicker stabilizer bars were added at both ends, six heavy-duty gas-charged shocks (two at the nose, four at the tail) were installed, and the power steering was revised to improve road feel. At the corners went 17x8 cast-aluminum wheels shod in P275/60HR17 Firestone Firehawk GTA tires. Brakes were 11.72-inch front discs, 11.03-inch rear drums.

Powering the 1993 Lightning was a 5.8-liter V-8, known previously as Ford's 351 Windsor small-block. But this wasn't your father's Windsor. Its cylinder heads were hot GT-40 cast-iron pieces with enlarged valves and high-flow ports. On top was the Cobra's 65mm throttle body bolted up to a two-piece GT-40 intake made up of a tubular aluminum upper section and a cast-aluminum bottom. Tubular stainless steel headers brought up

Modified with GT-40 hardware, the 1993 Lightning's electronically fuel-injected 351 cubic-inch V-8 produced 240 horsepower.

the exhaust end. Advertised output was 240 horsepower, a number many witnesses felt was fudged. With a four-speed automatic transmission and 4.10:1 gears standard, the Lightning was capable of 0–60 in 7.2 seconds, the quarter-mile in a tad more than 15 seconds.

According to a 1994 SVT release, this hot rod truck more or less represented "a Mustang GT with a cargo bed instead of a backseat." Its interior also was plusher than a typical F-150. A perforated leather steering wheel, custom-embroidered bucket seats (with power lumbar support, adjustable thigh support, and a power bolster on the

driver's side), and storage console all were standard. Only two exterior colors were offered, red and black. Production was 2,585 for the former, 2,691 for the latter.

Another 4,007 Lightning pickups followed in 1994, with the color breakdown reading 1,382 black, 1,165 red, and 1,460 for newly introduced white. Changes were minor, with additions including a driver's side air-bag and center high-mounted stop light on the back of the cab. New for 1995 was an "SVT" badge on the tail-gate. Lightning production this year was 2,280: 824 in black, 695 in red, and 761 in white.

After retiring in 1995, the SVT Lightning returned for 1999, this time with a more distinctive exterior led by a special front fascia with twin fog lamps. Production of 2001 Lightnings (shown here) was 6,381.

An SVT badge didn't appear on the Lightning's tailgate until 1995. The second-generation model also featured custom taillight treatments.

When the Lightning returned for 1999, it was powered by a 5.4-liter SOHC V-8 that was force fed by an Eaton Roots-type supercharger. Output was 360 horsepower. The 2001 Lightning's blown 5.4-liter V-8 (shown here) was tweaked up to 380 horsepower.

The Lightning temporarily faded away after 1995, but then returned for 1999 like a bolt out of the blue, this time with 360 very healthy horses. That was more than enough muscle to propel the second-generation SVT pickup from rest to 60 mph in a tidy 6.2 seconds—sensational performance considering this truck weighed nearly two-and-a-half tons.

Supplying those horses was a supercharged 5.4-liter single-overhead-cam (SOHC) Triton V-8 featuring a cast-iron block (a direct F-150 carryover) and alumi-num heads. Compression was a low 8.4:1 to compensate for the added boost supplied by an Eaton M112 Roots-type blower, which also incorporated an air-to-water intercooler. Special cooling was supplied for both water and oil, and the transmission was again a four-speed automatic. According to SVT tests, quarter-mile performance was 14.6 seconds at 97 mph.

Additional standard features included huge 18x9.5 cast-aluminum five-spoke wheels wearing 295/45ZR18 Goodyear Eagle F1-GS tires. Ride height was again low-

Second-generation Lightning interiors featured the SVT-trademark white-faced instrumentation.

ered (a half inch in front, two in back), and brakes were now four-wheel ABS discs, with the front rotors measuring 12.1 inches, the rears 13.1.

Completing the package was a more prominent image based on an F-150 Flareside body. Leading the way was a unique front fascia incorporating round driving lights akin to the Cobra Mustang. Rocker sill extensions ran down the sides to link the front fascia with the rear bumper, and the rocker molding on the right was cut out to allow twin 3.0-inch exhaust tips an exit into the atmosphere. Three clearcoated exterior finishes were offered: Bright Red, Black, and Oxford White. Leather touches and the SVT-signature white-faced gauge cluster went inside. A boost gauge to monitor the supercharger was included too.

Silver clearcoat paint became available for 2000 and

An Eaton supercharger was still huffing and puffing away in 2001, but it was joined by an enlarged mass-airflow-meter/air-intake combination to help produce twenty more horses.

Up to eight pounds of boost was supplied by the 2001 Lightning's Eaton blower.

mirrors were color-keyed instead of black. By the end of the year, sales of the blown Lightning totaled only 8,966 (4,000 in 1999, 4,966 for 2000), leaving SVT chief engineer John Coletti scrambling to enhance the attraction. His solution involved a little more here, a little more there.

"The 2001 SVT Lightning gives owners everything they have learned to love, but more of it," he said. "It's the most powerful, best-handling one we've yet produced, and some dramatic design changes make this model instantly recognizable. There'll be no mistaking it from previous SVT Lightning models, and now it's even more strongly differentiated from the standard F-150."

New wheels, a revamped front fascia, and trendy clear crystalline lenses weren't the only things setting the 2001 SVT Lightning apart from its forerunners. Behind that

aggressive-looking snout was 20 more horsepower that was delivered to the road via shorter rear gears: 3.73:1 compared to 3.55:1. An Eaton blower remained in place atop the Triton V-8, but it worked in concert with a few enlarged pieces (mass airflow meter and air intake opening) and a higher-flow intake manifold to produce those extra ponies.

The new 380-horsepower output figure not only looked impressive on paper, it also amounted to some serious real-world performance gains. Reportedly the time-honored 0–60 run needed only 5.8 seconds, while the quarter-mile went by in 13.9 ticks. Top end was listed at 142 mph—and remember, we're still talking about a pickup truck here.

Make that a world-class performance pickup. On August 13, 2003, a stone-stock Lightning scored an of-

Ford's Special Vehicle Team built various prototype toys over the years, including this Lightning-powered Ranger. Created in 2002, this hot little hauler was called the "Lightning Bolt." Not even a set of massive 345/35-18 tires in back could keep this machine from roasting its weenies.

ficial top speed of 147.7 mph at Ford's proving grounds in Romeo, Michigan, inspiring The Guinness Book of World Records people to anoint it the "World's Fastest Production Pickup Truck."

"We're proud to have certification from Guinness World records," said SVT marketing and sales manager Tom Scarpello. "It is a well-deserved record for the engineering team, and overdue confirmation to all the Lightning owners out there who have known for years that they drive the fastest truck on the planet."

"The SVT Lightning is just as stable and planted at 147 mph as it is at 55; only the scenery's going by faster," added SVT chassis systems supervisor Tom Chapman,

the driver who set the record. "That stability is a testament to the solid foundation of the Ford F-150, and the performance engineering found in SVT products."

Yearly changes again included paint choices as True Blue was unveiled for the 2002 Lightning, then replaced by Sonic Blue for 2003. Following the 6,381 Lightnings built for 2001 were 4,726 for 2002, 4,270 for 2003, and 3,871 for 2004. An exciting next-generation Lightning concept vehicle featuring 500 horsepower appeared in 2004, but rumors are all that remain now as far as continued production is concerned.

No worries, though. Continuing on after the Lightning subsided was another hopped-up F-150, this one created in conjunction with the Harley-Davidson motorcycle gang. Both legendary firms were born in 1903, and in March 1999 they announced a partnership to jointly develop and market exciting, limited-edition products, including machines to help mark their coinciding 100th anniversaries in 2003.

"This alliance brings together two of the most well-known and admired companies in the world," said Jeff Bleustein, Harley-Davidson chairman and CEO. "Ford and Harley-Davidson customers alike want a distinctive vehicle that makes a statement about themselves as individuals."

That vehicle, the 2000 Harley-Davidson F-150, was introduced on August 10, 1999, at the annual Sturgis Rally and Races event in Sturgis, South Dakota. "The Harley-Davidson F-150 is an exciting truck that has power and presence, symbolizing the 'Authentic American Muscle' tradition of both companies," said Ford Truck Vehicle Center vice president Gurminder S. Bedi during the unveiling. "Many Harley owners also own Ford Trucks. We believe they'll want to park this truck next to their prized Harley-Davidson motorcycle."

Dropped an inch in height and done only in black with familiar Harley-Davidson orange pinstriping, this customized Ford was based on an F-150 Extended Cab model with a Flareside cargo box crowned by a hard-shell tonneau cover. Massive 20x9 cast-aluminum five-spoke wheels (the first 20-inchers to come on a Ford vehicle) mounting P275/45VR20 Goodyear Eagle GTII tires, an SVT-style front valance with fog lamps, and chrome nurf bars below the rocker moldings announced the H-D F-150 in no uncertain terms. Interior features included black leather upholstery, a special dash ornament and a unique spun-metal instrument cluster. Power came from a 5.4-liter Triton V-8 that produced 260 horses.

A second-edition Harley-Davidson F-150 appeared for 2001, this time based on the roomier four-door SuperCab model. Another switch, to the SuperCrew body, came in 2003, and a new exterior color, Dark Shadow Gray, joined basic black this year. But the real

Stuffing about 400 horses worth of modified, supercharged 5.4-liter SOHC V-8 beneath the Lightning Bolt's hood wasn't all that tough, with relocated suspension components representing the most difficult surgery.

news involved upgrades made beneath the '03 H-D F-150's hood, where a detuned version of the Lightning's supercharged V-8 now resided. A slightly larger main blower-drive pulley translated into less boost to make sure the latest Harley-Davidson Ford didn't usurp on its SVT cousin's turf. Advertised output for the H-D F-150's blown 5.4-liter Triton was 340 horsepower, still nothing to huff at.

In March 1999, Ford officials and the Harley-Davidson motorcycle gang announced a partnership to co-develop specialty vehicles. The 2000 Harley-Davidson F-150 truck resulted from this deal. Offered first in Extended Cab form, the H-D F-150 became a four-door Super Cab model in 2001. It was switched to the Super Crew body (shown here) in 2003.

The Harley-Davidson edition moved up into the F-250 and F-350 4x4 Super Duty ranks for 2004, where it was powered by either a 6.8-liter Triton V-10 or 6.0-liter Power Stroke Diesel V-8. The familiar all-black and two-tone black-and-gray finishes carried on, but were completely overshadowed by a new combination of black over orange, a finish you simply couldn't miss.

A half-ton Harley-Davidson Ford returned for 2006 on Ford's latest, greatest F-150 platform and this time featured a naturally aspirated three-valve 5.4-liter Triton V-8 fitted with a specially tuned exhaust system that emitted a throatier roar. Output was 300 horsepower. Underneath was a sport handling suspension, and optional all-wheel-drive was available along with the tra-

ditional rear-drive powertrain. New too were even taller 22-inch wheels, yet another first for the F-150 family. Another new optional finish, this one done in Dark Amethyst, appeared for the 2007 H-D F-150.

The present Harley-Davidson interior is even more a work of art than before. "We've designed a cockpit that's a tribute to the open road," said F-Series chief designer Gordon Platto. "We've introduced high-gloss Piano Black cues along the instrument panel, center stack and console to bring in a feeling of visual motion. Combine that with the rich leather and bright chrome that's been such an essential part of all our Harley trucks, and you're surrounded with styling that salutes motorcycle culture."

Talk about an easy rider.

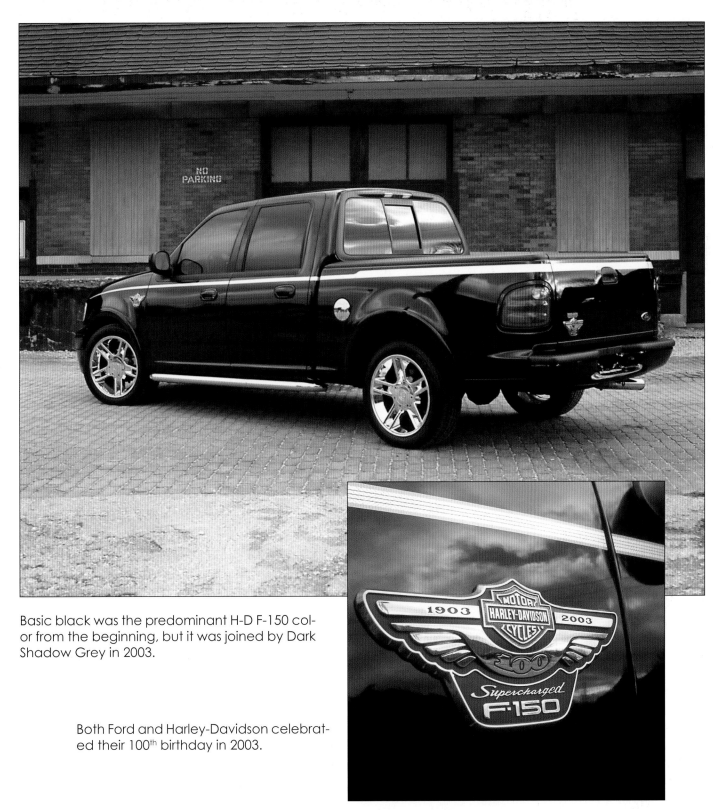

Basic black was the predominant H-D F-150 color from the beginning, but it was joined by Dark Shadow Grey in 2003.

Both Ford and Harley-Davidson celebrated their 100th birthday in 2003.

Initial power for the Harley-Davidson F-150 came from a 260-horse 5.4-liter Triton V-8 in 2000. For 2003, the H-D pickup was treated to a detuned version (shown here) of the SVT Lightning's supercharged V-8. Output was 340 horsepower.

Four captain's chairs and front and rear consoles came standard inside the 2003 H-D F-150. Full instrumentation and leather appointments were part of the deal, too.

Huge 20-inch chrome wheels were standard for the 2003 Harley-Davidson F-150 truck.

A luxurious leather interior was again a Harley-Davidson F-150 trademark in 2006.

The Harley-Davidson edition half-ton reappeared on Ford's new F-150 platform for 2006. Both two-wheel- and four-wheel-drive models were offered. A 300-horsepower 5.4-liter Triton V-8 was standard.

Dodge offered two half-ton chassis in 1965, one with a 114-inch wheelbase, the other at 122 inches. The Custom Sports Special, first seen the previous year, was offered on the longer frame. Racing stripes were part of the CSS deal. The 8-foot Sweptline cargo box (shown here) was standard; the mundane 7.5-foot Utiline box was an option.

Chapter Four
SPEED DEMONS: Dominating Dodges

Using the term "Big Three" when describing Detroit's long-running truck race was for years a misnomer. Chrysler Corporation's truck division for decades ranked a distant, distant third behind Chevrolet and Ford, with the former dominating the number one position from the Thirties into the Seventies, the latter doing the same for the last thirty years. "The Big Two and Dodge" was probably closer to the truth during the early postwar era, a time when International occasionally pushed the Mopar men down to fourth in annual sales rankings. Make that fifth during the Fifties thanks to a surging GMC, General Motors' other truck builder.

Dodge certainly got lost amidst some dark shadows a half century or so back. Its first truly new postwar pickup appeared in 1948, but barely anyone noticed thanks to Chevrolet's introduction of its cutting-edge Advance Design model the year before, followed closely by Ford's first F-series truck, also unveiled for 1948. The

A snazzy bucket-seat interior was standard inside the Custom Sports Special. A tachometer was added when the optional 426 V-8 was ordered.

Dodge's 225 cubic-inch slant-six was the base engine for the Custom Sports Special. Options included a 200-hosepower 318 cubic-inch V-8 or the top-dog 426 cubic-inch wedge-head V-8 (shown here). Chrome dress-up was included on the 426, which was rated at 365 horsepower.

Dodge truck boys actually beat their Bow-Tie counterparts to the punch with a modern overhead-valve V-8, announced in June 1954, but again garnered little fame. And when Dodge tried to join Chevy in Detroit's first playtoy pickup niche in 1957, its Cameo knockoff, the Sweptside, drew more guffaws than compliments.

So it only seems appropriate then that few witnesses today can recall Detroit's first muscle truck, introduced nearly 45 years ago by—you guessed it—the third player in the Big Three truck game. On February 9, 1964, Dodge announced its Custom Sports Special, available on 122-inch wheelbase D100 (half-ton) and D200 (3/4-ton) pickups with either a stylish Sweptline or traditional Utiline cargo box. On the outside, the CSS was dressed up with trendy racing stripes and extra chrome complements. Standard inside were bitchin' bucket seats (borrowed from a Dart GT), a center console (a Polara 500 unit) and rather plush carpeting that ran all the way from firewall to the top of the gas tank behind the seats.

Oak accents on the cargo box and tailgate were standard for Dodge's Li'l Red Truck in 1978 and 1979. Production of 1978 models (shown here) was 2,188. All were based on Dodge's D150 (115-inch wheelbase) half-ton fitted with a Utiline cargo box.

In base form this sporty pickup was by no means a tough customer. Standard was Dodge's 225 cubic-inch slant-six, rated at 140 horsepower. A 200-horse 318 cubic-inch V-8 was optional, but the real deal involved adding the 426-cid wedge-head big-block, which produced 365 horsepower. Included along with the potent 426 were power steering, dual exhausts, heavy-duty rear axle struts, a Load-Flite automatic transmission, and a tachometer. Only a handful of 426-equipped Custom Sports Specials were built for 1964 and 1965. The CSS package appeared again in 1966 but this time featured an optional 383 cubic-inch V-8 in place of the big, bad 426.

Ten years later Dodge came back with its "Adult Toys" collection. The first of these, the Street Van, was announced in March 1976. This cool, customized cruiser was followed soon by other special-edition models: the four-wheel-drive Macho, Ramcharger "Four by Four," and the Warlock pickup. Offered first in fad-conscious California, the Warlock officially joined the Adult Toys lineup in June that year after Chrysler officials determined that a "trick truck" craze was just gaining momentum in America.

"We were seeing an upswing in the number of people who want a light duty pickup instead of a second car,"

Standard wheels for the 1978 Li'l Red Truck measured 15x7 in the front, 15x8 out back. Standard tire sizes were GR60 at the nose, LR60 at the tail.

explained Dodge Truck sales manager Robert Kline. "We also were aware that more and more people were customizing and personalizing pickups, particularly the short wheelbase models. As with the van, the movement got its start on the West Coast and it's now moving across the country."

Adult Toys like the Warlock half-ton pickup were created to allow customers the chance to buy a pre-personalized vehicle directly from a Dodge dealer. Standard Warlock features included gold pinstriping, gold eight-spoke wheels, and oak sideboards atop the cargo box. Apparently all Dodge truck engines were available, beginning again with the 225-cid slant-six. V-8 options included the 318, 360, and 400, and some sources claim the 440 also found its way beneath a few Warlock hoods. This package was offered up through 1979, with the last

version called the "Warlock II."

In 1978 the Warlock was shoved aside by another Adult Toy, the flashier, more purposeful Li'l Red Express Truck. As the name implied, all of these hot Dodge pickups were painted red, and like the Warlock they featured ample gold pinstriping and oak accents out back. Twin big-rig-style exhaust stacks went behind the cab and chrome five-slot custom wheels were bolted on at the corners. Tires were fat 60-series Goodyear radials with raised white letters.

Beneath the hood was the real attraction: a high-performance 360 cubic-inch V-8 was the only engine offered for the Li'l Red Truck. Fed by an 850-cfm ThemoQuad four-barrel carburetor on a factory high-rise intake, this peppy small-block put out 225 net-rated horsepower. Delivering those ponies to the road was a

A dual-snorkel air cleaner and chrome complements were included with the Li'l Red Truck's standard 360 cubic-inch Higher Performance V-8. Output was 225 horsepower. Compression was 8.2:1.

beefed-up A-727 automatic transmission and a 3.55:1 Sure Grip differential.

Published performance figures included a quarter-mile run of 15.7 seconds at 88 mph for this playful pickup, making it one of America's meanest muscle machines at a time when "high" and "performance" had become dirty words around Detroit. Any wonder Dodge promoted this truck as "The Last American Hot Rod"?

Considering how few 426 Custom Sports Specials were built, it's probably more historically correct to credit the Li'l Red Truck for kicking off America's muscle truck legacy. This was definitely one hot half-ton,

and it inspired a relatively healthy following. Production in 1978 was 2,168, followed by another 5,118 in 1979. Some sources claim a 1980 model was marketed in Canada.

While nothing as hot as the Li'l Red Truck followed during the Eighties, Dodge remained no stranger to sporty imagery as far as its trucks were concerned. Then along came the all-new 1994 Ram pickup, a certifiably aggressive-looking machine that just begged to be muscled up and dressed out. A monochromatic Sport package, introduced late that year, took care of the dressing, while an optional V-10, made available midyear for

Rectangular headlights identified the 1979 Li'l Red Truck, of which 5,118 were built. New this year were 15x8 wheels wearing L60 rubber at all four corners.

heavier Rams, put 300 horses to work. An even snazzier SS/T package followed for Sport Rams with the 5.9-liter V-8 and featured 17-inch wheels, deep-throated exhausts, and Viper-like paint stripes.

Five years later the 1500-series (half-ton) Ram was treated to another new engine as Dodge truck engineers dusted off their fabled Hemi-head technology, last seen in legendary 426 cubic-inch form in 1971. Dis-placing 5.7 liters (345 cubic inches) this time around, Chrysler Corporation's reborn Hemi V-8 produced 345 horsepower, enough oomph to transform its light-duty pickup into a true hot rod hauler. Performance data, according to *Motor Trend*, included a 0–60 run in only 6.8 seconds for the 2003 Hemi Ram. The quarter-mile time was 15.11 seconds at 89.06 mph.

To appropriately accent all this newfound muscle,

A sporty Tuff steering wheel was standard inside the 1978 Li'l Red Truck, and this wheel carried over into early 1979 models (shown here). Later 1979 Li'l Red Trucks used a four-spoke deep-dish sport steering wheel.

Dodge in 2004 introduced a collection of high-profile dress-up packages: the short-bed Rumble Bee and GTX and their quad-cab running mate, the HemiSport. All, of course, came standard with the 345-horse Hemi V-8. The Rumble Bee received 20-inch wheels, lower body cladding and nostalgic striping reminiscent of Dodge muscle cars from days gone by. The GTX was specially striped too, in this case in remembrance of a Plymouth muscle car introduced in 1967. The HemiSport was offered in both two-wheel- and four-wheel-drive forms.

Yet another time machine debuted in 2005, this one appealing to NASCAR fans. "The all-new, limited-edition Dodge Ram Daytona has a bold, race-inspired attitude for customers seeking a performance-packaged pickup like no other," said Dodge marketing vice president Darryl Jackson. "The Ram Daytona will turn heads on the street and on the track."

Like Dodge's 1969 Charger Daytona, its 2005 Ram counterpart featured a high-flying wing in back, this time measuring 11 inches tall. Done in flat black, this spoiler also graphically commemorated the legendary muscle car that took to NASCAR speedways with a vengeance 36 years prior. Additional standard features included Hemi power, 20-inch chrome wheels, side-exiting Borla exhausts, and a numbered plaque on the dash.

Turning even more heads was Dodge's supreme muscle truck, the SRT-10, introduced in 2004. A product of Chrysler's Performance Vehicle Operations (PVO), this outrageous pickup was one of various "Street Racing Technology" models based on Mopar models, with the Viper SRT-10, introduced for 2003, leading the way. Creating the SRT truck was simple logic: the Viper's V-10 began life in Dodge truck ranks, why not send this monster mill back to its roots?

With 500 Viper horses beneath its functional hood scoop, the 2004 SRT-10 instantly became the hottest half-ton ever seen on this planet. Or any other. "The Ram SRT-10 is true to the performance ideals that created the original Viper," said Chrysler Group chief operating office Wolfgang Bernhard. "[It] delivers its astounding performance in a way that only Viper owners will recognize, with an endless rush of torque." Rest to 60 mph reportedly required a scant five clicks of the stopwatch, while the quarter-mile went by in a sizzling 13.62 seconds, topping out at 102.8 mph. As for top end…

Early in 2004 a stone-stock SRT-10 driven by 6-time NASCAR Craftsman Truck race winner Brendan Gaughn took to DaimlerChrysler's Proving Grounds in Chelsea, Michigan, in pursuit of the speed record established by Ford's SVT Lightning roughly six months before. Gaughn's two-lap average speed for the 4.71-mile oval was 154.587 mph, making the SRT-10 the new "World's Fastest Production Pickup Truck" according to the Guinness Book of World Records.

The Warlock was offered from 1976 to 1979 with a choice of power sources, from slant-six to V-8. Reportedly four colors were available: black, orange, red and green. Black was the most commonly seen finish.

"I've certainly driven some fast trucks, but I've certainly never experienced anything like setting a Guinness world record," said Gaughn. "I've known for a long time that the Dodge Ram is the ultimate truck for the race track, and this certainly proves the Ram SRT-10 is the ultimate performance truck for the street."

Along with its enormous, all-aluminum 8.3-liter V-10, the 2004 SRT-10 also featured a Hurst-shifted Tremec T56 six-speed manual transmission, a performance-tuned suspension with Bilstein shocks, 22-inch wheels wearing Pirelli Scorpion 305/40 tires, and ABS-equipped four-wheel discs. Front rotors measured 15 inches, the rears 14. Additional exterior enhancements included a front fascia with brake-cooling ducting and a fully functional rear spoiler that was removable to allow access to the cargo bed.

Updates included a special white-painted, blue-striped Commemorative Edition in 2005, issued to mark a dozen or so years of SRT activity at Chrysler. Commemorative SRT-4 (Neon) and SRT-10 Viper models

also were released in similar fashion that year. A four-door Quad Cab SRT-10 appeared for 2006. While all standard-cab SRT-10s featured six-speed manual transmissions, their Quad Cab counterparts were all fitted with four-speed automatics as part of a plan to give the Viper-powered Ram an actual trailer-towing capacity.

Whether or not a 500-horsepower performance pick-up should be towing a boat or such is your call. But working or playing, there's no question that the SRT-10 is king of the muscle truck world. So what if Dodge has always ranked third in sales. Chrysler's truck division clearly has lead the way many times over the years when it comes to building bad-to-the-bone half-ton haulers.

Powering the Li'l Red Express Dakota was Dodge's optional 3.9-liter V-6, rated at 125 horsepower.

Dodge's redesigned Ram pickup represented a sensation enough when it debuted for 1994. Then along came the Ram Sport late that year. Offered only in red at first, the Sport model featured a monochromatic exterior with large fog lamps up front. Black paint joined red in 1995. Shown here is a 1996 Ram Sport.

Another hot rod Ram appeared in 1996, this one honoring the Viper's appearance that year as the prestigious pace car for the Indianapolis 500. Based on a 1500 SLT Sport standard cab, the 1996 Indy 500 Special Edition featured 17-inch wheels and a 245-horsepower 5.9-liter V-8. It was painted to match the Viper GTS coupe.

All 2004 Rumble Bees were regular-cab/short-box models. Exteriors were either black with yellow stripes or yellow with black stripes. The yellow scoop on this Rumble Bee is a non-stock owner customization.

The Rumble Bee imagery was inspired by Dodge's "Scat Pack," a collection of muscle cars introduced in 1968. Among these was the Super Bee, a hopped-up Coronet adorned with this same speeding bumblebee.

RUMBLE BEE

Offered for 2004 and 2005, the GTX was similar to the Rumble Bee. Standard were 20-inch wheels and Hemi power beneath that big hood scoop. Available colors were Hemi Orange, Sublime Green, Plum Crazy Purple, and Banana Yellow.

MUSCLE TRUCKS

Like the Rumble Bee, the GTX package paid homage to a memorable Mopar muscle car, this one from Plymouth. First offered in 1967, the original GTX came standard with a 375-horsepower 440 cubic-inch big-block V-8.

Introduced in 2004, Dodge's SRT-10 quickly superseded Ford's SVT Lightning as the world's fastest production pickup. Top speed was 154 mph. A special Commemorative Edition SRT-10 (shown here) was introduced in 2005.

At 8.3 liters, the SRT-10's Viper-sourced V-10 was not only the biggest engine to ever hit light truck ranks in Detroit, it also was the most powerful. Maximum output was 500 horsepower at 5,600 rpm. Maximum torque was 525 lb.-ft.

All Viper beneath its hood, the SRT-10's V-10 featured aluminum construction for its block and heads. Heavy-duty cooling was also part of the package.

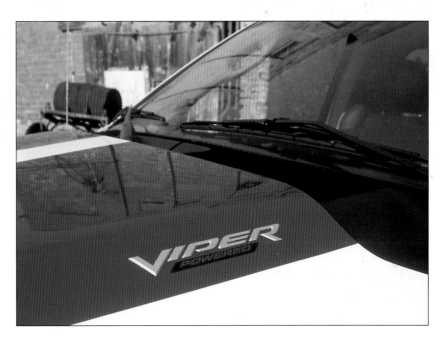

Commemorative Edition SRT-10 Dodges received a numbered plaque inside.

Bolstered leather bucket seats were standard inside the SRT-10. Standard-cab models also were fitted with Hurst shifters.

MUSCLE TRUCKS

A downright roomy Quad Cab SRT-10 (right) joined its standard-cab forerunner in 2006.

SRT people claimed the Viper truck's rear wing was fully functional, reducing some 165 pounds of aerodynamic lift at the tail at speed.

Introduced in 2005, the Ram Daytona was offered in two distinctive colors: Go Mango and Silver Metallic. A major hood scoop and 20-inch chrome wheels were standard, as were running boards for Quad-Cab models.

Body-colored guards were added to the 2005 Ram Daytona's grille and taillights. Though nowhere near as tall as the wing on a 1969 Charger Daytona, the Ram Daytona's 11-inch spoiler still stands out in a crowd.

Chrysler Corporation's Hemi roots date back to 1951. All Chrysler divisions save for Plymouth offered hemi-head power during the Fifties. The 426 Race Hemi then debuted for Dodge and Plymouth in 1964, followed by its Street Hemi counterpart in 1966. The last 426 Hemi was built in 1971. Hemi power reappeared in half-ton Dodge Ram ranks in 2003.

Like the Rumble Bee, the Ram Daytona came standard with the 5.7-liter Hemi V-8. At 345 horsepower, the Hemi makes any Dodge pickup a real stormer.

More great books from
Iconografix

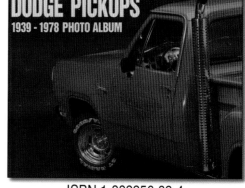

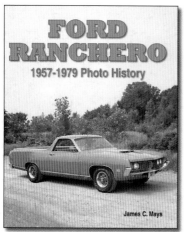

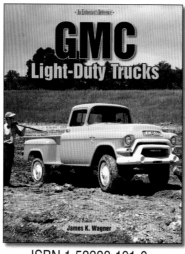

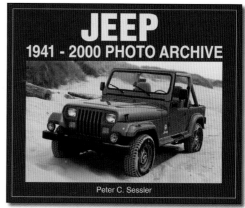

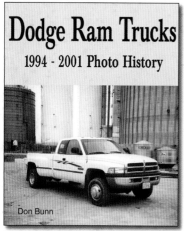

Iconografix, Inc.
P.O. Box 446, Dept BK,
Hudson, WI 54016
For a free catalog call: 1-800-289-3504
info@iconografixinc.com
www.iconografixinc.com